To: Eleanor From: Grammy and Grampy

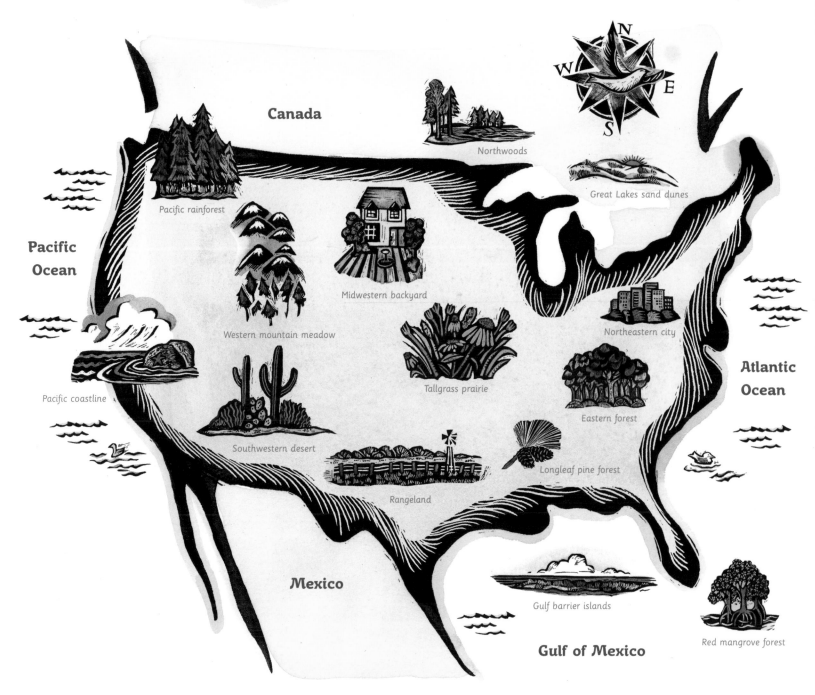

Canada

Northwoods

Great Lakes sand dunes

Pacific rainforest

Pacific Ocean

Midwestern backyard

Western mountain meadow

Northeastern city

Atlantic Ocean

Tallgrass prairie

Pacific coastline

Eastern forest

Southwestern desert

Longleaf pine forest

Rangeland

Mexico

Gulf barrier islands

Red mangrove forest

Gulf of Mexico

Many birds—more than 500 kinds—live in habitats all over the United States.

Claudia McGehee

Where Do Birds Live?

UNIVERSITY OF IOWA PRESS, IOWA CITY

Thanks to all who contributed their knowledge and passion to this book, especially Julian Avery, Holly Carver, Jim Dinsmore, James and Barbara Leupold, and Jim and Jean Sandrock

Thank you to my family and friends for love and support and to the birds of Bluffwood Lane for daily inspiration

A Bur Oak Book

University of Iowa Press, Iowa City 52242
Copyright © 2010 by Claudia McGehee
www.uiowapress.org
Prepress by iocolor, Seattle
Manufactured in China
by C&C Offset Printing Co., Ltd.
Shenzhen, Guangdong Province
Job # HK2143

Design by Kristina Kachele Design, llc

The University of Iowa Press is a member of Green Press Initiative and is committed to preserving natural resources.

Printed with reinforced binding on acid-free paper

CIP data on file with the Library of Congress

Page 1: Henslow's sparrow, page 2: western tanager, page 3: cedar waxwing, page 32: yellow-breasted chat

To Dan,
the early bird

Forebird

Hundreds of different kinds of birds live among us. Some are tiny, like the Anna's hummingbird, which weighs no more than a penny. Some are huge, like the California condor, which has wings that spread as wide as a car. Some wade in marshy waters, like the great blue heron. Others scratch in desert sand, like the Gambel's quail. Some eat bugs and seeds. Some eat lizards and snakes.

The size and sound of a bird, the shape of its bill, the color of its feathers, the way it builds its nest, and the kinds of things it eats make each bird special. These are all the "what" of birds. What about the "where" of birds? Where do birds live?

Choosing the right home is very important for birds. Birds live where they can find the type of food, shelter, and climate that is best for them. These places are called habitats. Habitats can be small, like a lake or a tree or a neighborhood park. They can also be large, like a whole forest or a mountain range. Most habitats change with each season, becoming warmer or colder, wetter or dryer. By migrating, flying north in the spring and south in the fall, many birds live in more than one habitat during the year.

This book looks at fourteen habitats where birds live in the summer months. Some places may be far away from your home; others may be very close, perhaps right in your own backyard. Wherever they live, birds are a fascinating part of our world.

Tallgrass Prairie
Bobolink

Look out over a tallgrass prairie on a breezy summer day. The gently waving grasses and wildflowers that make up the prairie move like ocean waves. There are very few trees, but some prairie plants grow more than eight feet high. Rich soil and the right amount of rain and sunshine give tallgrass prairies all they need to thrive. This wide-open grassland is an ideal habitat for a songbird like the bobolink.

If you spy a small bird with a white back, an all-black underbelly, and a cream-colored cap on its head, it's a male bobolink.

Bobolinks eat the seeds and insects found in the open prairie spaces. They build grassy nests on the ground. The bobolink's nest and egg color blend well with its surroundings to keep the young birds hidden.

Bobolink ground nests are difficult to see.

Because prairies don't have many trees to perch on, a number of prairie birds sing as they fly. Bobolinks pour out lovely liquid songs as they soar above the grasses.

Tallgrass prairies once grew across a large area in the middle of North America. Now, most have been plowed under and replaced by farms and cities. Fortunately, many people are preserving the tallgrass prairies that remain, and in some places, they are planting new prairies. You can visit some of these prairies. Where there are prairies, there will be homes for bobolinks.

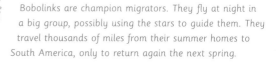

Bobolinks are champion migrators. They fly at night in a big group, possibly using the stars to guide them. They travel thousands of miles from their summer homes to South America, only to return again the next spring.

Other residents: plains pocket mouse, regal fritillary, katydid, greater prairie-chicken, upland sandpiper, American badger

Western Mountain Meadow Mountain Bluebird

In ancient times, powerful natural pressures underneath the earth's surface pushed and folded the land above. Over hundreds of years, glaciers—huge, grinding plates of ice—and rivers carved out canyons and gorges and the rugged mountain ranges we see today. Many habitats are found here, from treeless mountaintops to the thick forests and open meadows below.

The mountain bluebird, a fast-flying little songbird, lives near mountain meadows. If a flash of bright sky-blue streaks by, you've probably seen an adult male bluebird.

In the meadows, bluebirds find insects to eat. When it is time to nest, they fly to the forest edge to look for trees with holes in their trunks.

Bluebirds migrate south to warmer places for the winter at the same time that the leaves on the aspen trees turn golden.

As more people cut down trees and build houses near mountains, bluebirds find it harder to locate places to nest. If you live close to a mountain meadow, you can help by building nest boxes for bluebirds.

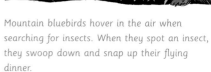

Mountain bluebirds hover in the air when searching for insects. When they spot an insect, they swoop down and snap up their flying dinner.

The opening in a nest box must be the right size for bluebirds, so other birds don't nest there instead.

Other residents: yellow-bellied marmot, Clark's nutcracker, blue grouse, moose, golden eagle

The Pacific rainforest is properly named—it is one of the rainiest places in the United States. Majestic fir, cedar, hemlock, and spruce trees grow in the rainforest. These evergreen trees keep their green needles all year long and make cones for seeds. Not much sunshine gets through the thick forest top, but thousands of plants and animals that like moist shade and mild weather flourish here.

Within the sound of ocean waves, the common raven lives in the lush green rainforest. You can easily observe these large birds with their strong powerful legs and wedge-shaped tails. Both male and female ravens have glossy black bodies and shaggy throat feathers. They are omnivorous, which means they eat both plants and animals.

Ravens are social birds that use many different calls to communicate with each other.

Because of their parents' size and intelligence, raven chicks rarely get picked on by other birds.

They build deep, bowl-shaped nests high in the tall evergreens. The nests are lined with animal fur to keep their eggs and chicks warm.

Once, rainforests covered wide areas of the Pacific Northwest, but much of the original rainforest has been cut down and logged. Little is left outside protected parks. You can explore the habitat that ravens call home all year round when you visit these rainforest parks.

Full of personality, ravens make graceful tumbling moves in the air. When they are on the ground, ravens walk instead of hop, like most other birds do.

Pacific Rainforest
Common Raven

Many Native American groups like the Tlingit, Haida, and Tsimshian also call the rainforest home. They use ravens in their artworks and stories, calling the raven Trickster because it does clever things.

Other residents: Douglas squirrel, western tailed blue, banana slug, varied thrush,
Roosevelt elk, spotted owl, marbled murrelet, chestnut-backed chickadee

Where land and sea meet, expect to find interesting habitats. Cliffs carved by the force of waves beating against rocks make perfect homes for birds that eat fish and shellfish.

Black oystercatchers are large shorebirds that live along rocky coastlines. They have all-black bodies, yellow eyes, light pink legs, and long orange bills. When you walk on a beach, you can hear them noisily peeping as they look for food along the water's edge. Sometimes their call sounds like a whistle.

Oystercatchers make nests called scrapes in shallow dents along the rocky beach. The parent birds line the nest with small shells and pebbles. When the eggs hatch, both parents care for the chicks until they can fly. Most black oystercatchers live all year round where they nest.

When oil from big ships and garbage spill into the ocean, the black oystercatcher's home is in danger. Keeping the ocean and beach clean is most important to the birds that live along the coast.

Pacific Coastline
Black Oystercatcher

Sometimes names are misleading. Black oystercatchers don't catch oysters. They pry open other kinds of shellfish with their strong beaks. They also wade in the surf, hoping to find shells that have already popped apart.

Limpets, barnacles, and mussels that cling to rocks are some of the black oystercatcher's favorite foods.

Other residents: elephant seal, California gull, semipalmated plover, limpet, snowy plover

The deserts of the southwestern United States are covered with sand and rocks and plants that don't need much water. The desert gets almost no rain. It stays dry and hot during the day for most of the year, but at night it can get very cold. The tall saguaro cactus is one symbol of the desert. The greater roadrunner is another.

The greater roadrunner is a long-legged, large-beaked bird that can run up to 17 miles per hour on the flat, open desert. You can recognize this speedy bird by its shaggy head crest and long, white-tipped tail, if you are lucky enough to see one standing still.

Roadrunners can fly, but they prefer to run as they hunt for food. They trot quickly, looking for bugs, lizards, and snakes to eat. When they spot their prey, they speed up to catch it.

Roadrunner parents make a platform nest of sticks in the lower branches of a shrub or cactus to help their eggs and chicks stay warm in the nighttime chill.

Roadrunners need a lot of space to run and hunt. It's important to keep open desert free from houses and highways as much as possible, so roadrunners can have all the space they need.

Roadrunners will chase prey.

Southwestern Desert
Greater Roadrunner

The male roadrunner moves his head crest up and down.

Roadrunners belong to a family of birds in which two toes point forward and two point backward. A roadrunner makes X-shaped prints in the sand.

Other residents: zebra-tailed lizard, black-tailed jackrabbit, coyote, cactus wren, Arizona desert scorpion, elf owl, Gila woodpecker, Gila monster, Gambel's quail

Rangeland
Scissor-tailed Flycatcher

Rangeland is open, rolling grassland that is used for grazing cattle, horses, and sheep in the lower western United States. Divided with fencing to keep livestock in certain spaces, rangeland is also used by wildlife that have learned to adapt to human activity. The scissor-tailed flycatcher spends its summers in this wide-open habitat.

The scissor-tailed flycatcher is named for the shape of the male's forked tail. You'll see how his very long tail feathers open in mid-air, like a pair of scissors, when he flies to attract a mate.

Insects common to rangeland, like grasshoppers, crickets, and beetles, are the scissor-tail's favorite foods. Farmers and ranchers think highly of the scissor-tail for helping them control these crop-eating bugs.

When building their nests, scissor-tails often use string, bits of paper, and cloth.

Without proper management, unwanted trees quickly crowd out the rangeland's native grasses and wildflowers, making it harder for animals to find food. Although fires are dangerous in many situations, human-managed fires control invading trees and help birds like the scissor-tail thrive on the rangeland.

Large flocks of more than fifty scissor-tails congregate before and during migration.

Strong thunderstorms and high winds that occur during the scissor-tail's nesting season make it hard for the parents to protect the baby birds.

Other residents: northern bobwhite, cattle egret, Angus cattle, Swainson's hawk

Gulf Barrier Islands
Brown Pelican

Many long, sandy islands dot the coast of the southern United States. Pushed by wind and waves, sand builds up over time to create these island habitats. Seeds float in, blow in, or are dropped by birds. They lodge in the sand and emerge as grasses and other plants.

These barrier islands protect the main coastline from the full force of strong storms and hurricanes. They are also home to many kinds of ocean birds, like the brown pelican. Brown pelicans are large, dark-bodied birds with white necks, stubby legs, big webbed feet, and hooked beaks with special stretchy pouches that work like fishing nets. You will notice their large beaks first.

Brown pelicans are very social. They nest in groups called colonies. They do almost everything together—roosting, raising their families, flying in formation, and fishing. They sometimes nest on sandy ground in between marsh grasses. Both parents build the nest and take care of the chicks.

In the past, chemicals used by people to control weeds ended up in the fish that brown pelicans ate. This made the eggs of brown pelicans very breakable, and not many chicks survived. A ban on these dangerous poisons has allowed the pelican to patrol the barrier islands in greater numbers again. In fact, once considered an endangered species, brown pelicans are now plentiful.

Gliding and flapping in a line over the water, brown pelicans search for fish. When they spot one, they turn steeply downward, fold their bodies like paper airplanes, and plunge into the water. Their bills open to scoop up fish with one big sweep.

Younger brown pelicans also fish while floating.

Other residents: Texas diamondback terrapin, laughing gull, tricolored heron

Longleaf Pine Forest Red-cockaded Woodpecker

A cockade is a ribbon worn to decorate a hat. The male woodpecker's cockade, a small area of red feathers on the side of his head, is hard to see from far away.

In the southern forests of the United States, tall longleaf pine trees grow far enough apart to let sunshine in. This light lets grasses, shrubs, and wildflowers grow well underneath the trees, creating a park-like habitat.

The red-cockaded woodpecker is a rare bird that can live only in longleaf pine forests. If you're lucky and sharp-eyed while you're walking in these woods, you might see its black-and-white zebra back, black head cap, and white cheeks.

The male woodpecker chooses a large, living pine tree, usually eighty years old or more, to nest in. With his strong beak, he hollows out a hole in the trunk. As he chips away at the tree bark, his hooked claws help him climb and hold on, and his stiff tail helps him balance. Sticky tree sap dripping from the nest cavity helps keep squirrels and snakes away.

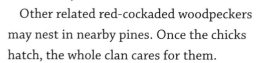

A red-cockaded woodpecker scouts for a good nesting tree.

Other related red-cockaded woodpeckers may nest in nearby pines. Once the chicks hatch, the whole clan cares for them.

Longleaf pine trees once covered a large area of the southern United States. Most of these trees have been cut down, and the red-cockaded woodpecker can't find enough older trees to nest in. Survival for this woodpecker will depend on protecting the forests that remain.

Other residents: fox squirrel, eastern towhee, Bachman's sparrow, gopher tortoise

Found between land and sea, red mangrove trees live in salty water. Thanks to their design, the mangroves' roots block salt from entering the tree, letting only fresh water in. Their long, arched roots reach deep down through the water, creating a good place for small fish to hide. This is why the mangrove forest is an excellent habitat for fish-eating birds like the roseate spoonbill.

There are many unusual features on a roseate spoonbill. If you see one, the first thing you'll notice is its bright pink body and red shoulders. With its long, flat, spoon-shaped bill and pale green bald head, the spoonbill is a most interesting bird.

Spoonbills live and nest in large colonies. Their nesting areas, called rookeries, are found high in the branches of the mangrove trees. Each nest, about the size of a stop sign, is sturdily built of twigs and sticks. Both parents sit on the eggs, and both feed the chicks after the eggs hatch.

For the spoonbill, it has not been easy being pink. A hundred years ago, their feathers were used to decorate women's hats; collectors hunted these gentle birds until they nearly disappeared. Laws were made to protect these beautiful birds. Today, as more and more mangrove forests are cut down to make room for houses, the roseate spoonbill is threatened again.

Red Mangrove Forest
Roseate Spoonbill

Spoonbills fly with their necks and legs stretched out. Their long, broad wings allow them to glide in between flaps.

Spoonbills wade in shallow water, sweeping their bills from side to side in search of fish, shrimp, water bugs, and other food. They have an especially sensitive bill that helps them feel out fish and other prey. Spoonbills are fond of shrimp, which give this bird its pink feathers.

Other residents: manatee, mangrove salt marsh snake, wood stork, jackfish, mangrove skipper

Forests of the eastern United States can be warm and humid in the summer and snowy and cold in the winter. The leaves of many of the trees that grow here are deciduous; they change color and drop off in the fall. If you walk through an eastern forest on a summer day, you will see and hear many signs of life. Wildlife make their homes on every level in the forest, from moles that dig underground burrows to songbirds that nest high in the treetops. American redstarts build their nests and forage for insects in the protection of the tall oaks, beeches, and maples.

Catch a glimpse of the male American redstart, and you'll know why he is called the butterfly of the bird world. His black body and bright orange wing and tail patches and the quick, fluttery way he flies will remind you of this colorful insect. The female, a less flashy olive-brown, also flits and flutters like a butterfly.

The eastern forest is too cold in the winter for redstarts. They migrate to the lowlands of South America and stay until spring, when they return north to their summer eastern forest home.

When people cut down trees, the small patches that are left can't offer enough food and shelter for the wide variety of birds and animals that live here. Finding ways to reconnect the forest patches will give American redstarts a future as bright as their feathers.

Eastern Forest
American Redstart

The American redstart's scientific name, Setophaga ruticilla, means "moth-eating redtail." Forest-dwelling moths like this Io moth can end up being a redstart's meal.

A male redstart flashes his orange tail and wing patches to surprise insects.

Other residents: eastern wood-pewee, ovenbird, American black bear, eastern screech-owl, Virginia opossum, woodland salamander, orb weaver spider

You might not think that birds could live in a place filled with hundreds of tall buildings and miles of streets and sidewalks. Think again. A surprising number of birds have adapted to urban life.

Parks with large trees and lots of green grass are often nestled in the middle of this busy environment. If the park has a pond, ducks will almost certainly be floating on it.

Mallards are a common duck of city parks. You can easily identify the male mallard during nesting season by his glossy green head and white neck ring. Females are mostly light brown with a brilliant purple-blue feathered area on their wings.

Mallards eat all sorts of pond plants and insects as well as seeds and acorns. They make shallow nests of grasses and reeds on the ground near the water.

The mallard has easily adapted to city park life. For many other birds, it is tougher. Birds tend to migrate at night, but the bright lights of cities confuse them. Some, sadly, fly into windows and injure themselves. Some big cities dim the lights of their tall buildings during bird migration in the spring and fall. A darkened city skyline helps save thousands of birds every year. These actions will make sure that you continue to see lots of different birds along with mallards in city parks.

Mallards are dabbling ducks. While swimming, they search for food in shallow water. When they spot something edible, they tip their tails up and dabble, plunging their heads into the water and reaching with their bills for dinner below.

Northeastern City
Mallard

Mallard parents can have as many as thirteen ducklings. Soon after they hatch, the young birds are able to swim and feed themselves, although they stay close to their mother for protection for weeks.

Other residents: black-crowned night-heron, Canada goose, pied-billed grebe, red-tailed hawk

Great Lakes Sand Dunes
Herring Gull

Herring gulls are impressive characters with their flat heads and large bills. Adults have red spots on the bottom of their lower beaks during nesting season.

Thousands of years ago, water melting from glaciers sculpted and filled the Great Lakes. Sand along lake beaches was blown by the wind into dunes, which continue to be reshaped by the wind even today. Birds and animals thrive among these sand dunes, sparkling lakes, and long shorelines. Low-growing plants and nearby woodland trees provide food, shelter, and nesting opportunities for all sorts of birdlife. The stocky herring gull is one of the largest of the gulls that live here. Look for its white and speckled gray body, light pink legs, and yellow eyes.

Herring gulls line their scrape nests with pebbles, seashells, feathers, and grasses. They live and nest in big colonies, usually on islands, with other herring gulls. Young chicks sometimes play tug-of-war with each other.

The omnivorous herring gulls hunt along the water's edge for seaweed and fish. Because herring gulls are scavengers, their eating habits benefit humans. Herring gulls eat dead fish, keeping beaches cleaner. They also lead fishing boats to places where herring fish swim, earning them their name.

Herring gulls prefer to drink fresh water, but if they need to, they can drink salt water. Glands located over their eyes filter out the salt. Herring gulls can live to be thirty years old, which is longer than many birds live.

Because of climate change, the Great Lakes are getting warmer. What will this mean to the fish, animals, and birds that live here? Scientists are studying these changes to learn more.

Other residents: white-footed mouse, bank swallow, killdeer, piping plover

Northwoods
Scarlet Tanager

Lakes, marshes, and other waterways abound in the northwoods of the Upper Midwest. Smooth rock shorelines are fringed with a mixture of evergreen and leafy deciduous trees, creating a unique place for animals to live.

When you hike through the northwoods, be sure to look up as well as around. You may spot one forest songbird, the scarlet tanager. It lives high in the tree canopy, quietly searching for insects. The male scarlet tanager is a bright scarlet-red, with black wings and tail. The female is a soft olive-green.

Short and cool summers change into long and cold winters in the northwoods. It is too chilly and there is not enough food for scarlet tanagers to stay year round. They migrate all the way to South America each fall.

Extensive logging in this habitat has threatened the waterways and removed trees that many animals and birds depend on. People are working to conserve the northwoods so birds like the scarlet tanager can continue to summer here.

Even though the males are brightly colored, they can easily hide in the treetops' filtered sunlight.

Every year, thousands of birds like the scarlet tanager are banded by researchers trained to capture, identify, weigh, measure, and release them. The band has a number on it that identifies the bird. Banding helps scientists learn more about birds. Every year, many people volunteer to help scientists band birds. You can, too!

Other residents: bobcat, common loon, bald eagle, eastern chipmunk

Perhaps the most important bird habitat is the one closest to where *you* live. Whether in a city or a small town or out in the country, backyard trees and shrubs can shelter birds and other animals. Flowers, grasses, fruit trees, and berry bushes are important food sources. Where you live determines what kinds of birds live there. The ruby-throated hummingbird is one kind of bird that zips around midwestern backyards.

Ruby-throated hummingbirds have metallic green bodies that are about the size of your thumb. They also have shimmering feathers. Males have beautiful ruby-red throats that look purple in sunlight. They fly so fast that their wings are just a blur.

All kinds of hummingbirds are attracted to flower gardens, where lots of insects hang out. Along with insects, hummingbirds feed on flower nectar, which they collect with their long tongues. They also eat spiders from webs.

Hummingbirds have such tiny feet that they can't walk or hop. Instead, they shuffle along on tree branches. Hummingbirds don't stay in the Midwest after summer. Come fall, they use their little wings to fly all the way to South America.

Although they seem as if they are constantly moving, hummingbirds also perch and rest.

Midwestern Backyard
Ruby-throated
Hummingbird

Ruby-throated hummingbird nests, about as big as a walnut, are made from mud, tree bark, plant fibers, and even spider webs. The eggs look like little white peas.

The sphinx moth looks and behaves much like a hummingbird. These large daytime insects dart around quickly, then hover in mid-air to gather nectar from flowers with their long proboscis, their feeding tube. How do you tell the difference between this unusual moth and a hummingbird? Hummingbirds don't let you get too close. And if you see brown stripes on the back, it's a sphinx moth.

Other residents: white-breasted nuthatch, gray squirrel, cicada, blue jay, northern cardinal, American robin, gray catbird, chipping sparrow, American goldfinch

Afterbird

As more and more natural habitats disappear, some birds rely on backyards to find food and nest sites. You can help make your backyard the best possible home for birds.

• Create a feeding station for birds. Some birds like to eat seed from the ground. Others perch and pick from hanging feeders. Find out what birds come to your backyard, and fill different feeders to encourage all kinds of birds.

• A birdbath or fountain gives birds water to drink. Close-by trees and bushes provide safe places that birds can fly to if danger approaches. If you don't have a tree in your backyard, put a branch, or anything birds can perch on, close to the feeding station.

• Keeping cats indoors could save hundreds of thousands of birds each year.

• Place safety stickers on windows to prevent birds from crashing into the glass.

• Field binoculars, special glasses that help you see birds up close while you stand farther away, are fun to use. Field guides are books that include illustrations to help you identify the birds you see.

• Make notes about the birds you see. Besides color and shape, what else is different about each bird? Its song? The way it holds its tail? How it acts around other birds?

• Share what you learn with your friends and family. Make it an adventure to watch birds together.

Most of all, celebrate where birds live; it's where you live, too!

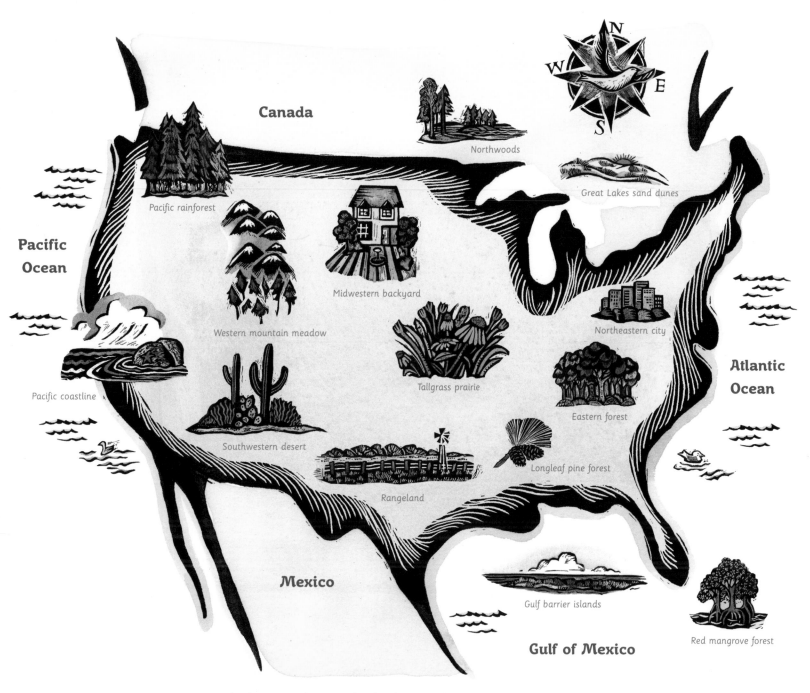

Canada

Northwoods

N
W   E
S

Great Lakes sand dunes

Pacific rainforest

Pacific
Ocean

Midwestern backyard

Western mountain meadow

Northeastern city

Tallgrass prairie

Pacific coastline

Atlantic
Ocean

Southwestern desert

Eastern forest

Longleaf pine forest

Rangeland

Mexico

Gulf barrier islands

Red mangrove forest

Gulf of Mexico

Many birds—more than 500 kinds—live in habitats all over the United States.